Who or What Is the Prophetic Beast?

Who or what is "the wild Beast" of the Apocalypse, or book of Revelation, chapters 13 and 17? What does Bible prophecy reveal about world events now leading to Armageddon and the end of this age? This two-part booklet deals with governments and wars that will bring this world to its final end. *pg. 38 & 39*

Original text by Herbert W. Armstrong (1892-1986)
Part One: ©1960 Worldwide Church of God
Part Two: ©1952 Worldwide Church of God
Cover illustration by C. Winston Taylor
All Rights Reserved
Printed in U.S.A.

ISBN 0-943093-96-1

WHO OR WHAT IS THE PROPHETIC BEAST?

BIBLE PROPHECY reveals events of our time—world-shaking events soon to change your life. Major world-shaking events are foretold in symbolic language about a mysterious world-dominating wild beast described in Revelation 13 and 17.

Is the beast a mysterious superman world dictator yet to appear? ... Is he the Antichrist? ... or a government? ... or a church?

THE MOST important question of the hour is *what,* or *who,* is the BEAST, the IMAGE of the beast, and the MARK of the beast spoken of in the Apocalypse or book of Revelation?

Whatever this weird beast—whatever the baffling image—whatever the mysterious mark—it behooves you and me to find out!

For it is those of this very present generation who shall be worshiping this beast or his image, or shall have received his mark, that will suffer the unspeakable torture of the seven last plagues!

Ignorance will not excuse! "My people are destroyed for lack of knowledge," says the Eternal, in Hosea 4:6. And the illustration of Ezekiel's watchman shows that those who are unaware, because they are not warned, will suffer just the same (Ezek. 33:6; and 3:18). God expects the spiritual leader of His people to be His "watchman" (Ezek. 33:7) and to warn the people.

Who Shall Suffer the PLAGUES?

Listen! John in the Apocalypse or book of Revelation describes the last warning message: "If any man worship the beast and his image, and receive his mark in his forehead, or in his hand, the same shall drink of the wine of the wrath of God, which is poured out without mixture" (Rev. 14:9, 10). This prophecy is most significant because it is revealing, in advance, events immediately ahead of us at this present time.

Listen again!

John, carried forward in vision into the terrible "day of the Lord," sees these plagues beginning to fall! "And the seven angels came out of the temple, having the seven last plagues . . . and the first went, and poured out his vial upon the earth; and there fell a noisome and grievous sore upon the men which had the mark of the beast, and upon them which worshipped his image" (Rev. 15:6 and 16:2).

Every sign tells us these things will happen, plunging the world into the most frantic, frenzied state of anguish ever known, almost certainly within a matter of the next several years!

Those who suffer the wrath of Almighty God are described as those who worship the beast, or his image, or have his mark.

It is futile to try to imagine, as so many are doing, what the mark of the beast may be. These prophecies are real. They are imminent. Because these and other prophecies have never been understood until now, even churches, the theologians, evangelists have been ignoring prophecies in general and these imminent prophecies in particular. Too many are trying to speculate in their imaginations. But God says, "My thoughts are not your thoughts" (Isa. 55:8).

We can't work this out in our minds. We are face to face with a stern reality, not an imaginary fairy tale! There is only one way to learn the truth. That is to study carefully, cautiously, prayerfully, with an open mind yielded to and guided by the Holy Spirit, all the testimony of all the scriptures that bear on this question.

We cannot determine what the mark of the beast may be, until we have learned what, or who, the beast is!

For, of course, the mark is the beast's mark. Who, what then, is the beast?

The Bible DESCRIPTION
of the BEAST

The beast, the image of the beast and the mark of the beast are all described primarily in the 13th chapter of the book of Revelation.

Notice carefully this Bible description. The apostle John was being given this message for you and me of this day. In the vision he saw "a beast rise up out of the sea, having seven heads and ten horns, and upon his horns ten crowns, and upon his heads the name of blasphemy."

"And the beast which I saw was like unto a leopard, and his feet were as the feet of a bear, and his mouth as the mouth of a lion: and the dragon gave him his power, and his seat, and great authority" (Rev. 13:1-2).

Now most of those who are teaching and preaching to others on these subjects overlook entirely this description. For this description will IDENTIFY the beast.

If the beast is some mysterious superman, or antichrist, soon to appear as world dictator, he will be a peculiar-looking individual indeed, for he will have seven heads, and ten horns! Have you ever seen a man with seven heads, and ten horns growing out of one of his heads? And did you ever see a man who was like a leopard, and can you imagine a superman coming who will have the feet of a bear, and the mouth of a lion? And will he appear by coming up out of some ocean?

Now these, of course, are all symbols. The very word *beast* is a symbol. And our problem is to interpret the symbols, for they stand for real, literal things. But man cannot interpret biblical symbols. And when we know what the heads and the horns are, what the feet of the bear, the mouth of the lion, and likeness to a leopard all mean, then we can know what, or who, the beast really is!

The Bible Interprets Its Own Symbols

The point we want to stress is that the Bible interprets its own symbols! If we want the truth, we must be guided solely by the Bible interpretation, not man's interpretations and imaginations.

And the Bible itself tells us what they represent!

In the 7th chapter of Daniel, we find exactly these same symbols described. Here again are the beasts, the seven heads, the ten horns, and here also is the lion, the bear, and the leopard. And here the Bible tells us what these symbols represent.

God had given Daniel understanding in dreams and visions (Dan. 1:17). And Daniel had a dream and a vision (Dan. 7:1) in which he saw four great beasts (verse 3). And notice, as in Revelation, the beasts came up out of the sea.

The first was like a "lion" (verse 4), the second like a "bear" (verse 5), the third like a "leopard" (verse 6), and the fourth was so dreadful and terrible it could not be compared to any wild beast known to inhabit the earth (verse 7)!

Now there was only one head described on the lion, one for the bear, one for the fourth beast—but the third beast, the leopard, had four heads—thus making seven heads in all! And out of this great and dreadful fourth beast grew ten horns!

Now notice verse 16, latter part. Here comes the interpretation of the things! The question is, will we accept this Bible interpretation of the seven heads, the ten horns, the lion, the bear and the leopard?

"These great beasts, which are four, are four kings which shall arise out of the earth," is the interpretation of verse 17.

And the word *king* is synonymous with kingdom, and used only in the sense that the king represents the kingdom over which he rules, for in verse 23 we read, "The fourth beast shall be the fourth kingdom upon the earth." Notice also the word *kingdom* is used to explain the beasts in verses 18, 22, 24, and 27.

Now what do the "horns" represent? Notice verse 24: "And the ten horns out of this kingdom are ten kings that shall arise." Notice the ten horns, or ten succeeding kingdoms or governments, come OUT OF A KINGDOM, not out of a man, or a superman. This alone makes plain that the beast is not some mysterious personal superman yet to come. Also that the beast is not a church as some claim, for no ten kingdoms ever did, or will, come out of a church. And since "king" in these prophecies only stands for the kingdom he represents, and since the words are used interchangeably, it follows that these ten horns are ten succeeding kingdoms growing out of the fourth kingdom, which was to rule the earth!

Identification of the Kingdoms

These same four world-ruling gentile kingdoms are described in the second chapter of Daniel. King Nebuchadnezzar of the Chaldean Empire, who had taken the Jews captive, had a dream, the meaning of which God revealed to Daniel.

The dream is described in verses 31-35. The king saw a great image. Its head was of gold, its breast and arms of silver, its belly and thighs of brass, its legs of iron and its feet and toes were part iron and part clay. Finally, a stone, not in men's hands, but supernaturally, smote the image upon his feet and toes. It was broken in pieces and was blown away like chaff. Then the stone that smashed it became a great mountain and filled the whole earth.

"This," Daniel says, beginning verse 36, "is the dream; and we will tell the interpretation thereof before the king."

". . . Thou art this head of gold. And after thee shall arise another kingdom inferior to thee, and another third kingdom of brass, which shall bear rule over all the earth. And the fourth kingdom shall be strong as iron: forasmuch as iron breaketh in pieces and subdueth all things: and as iron that breaketh all these, shall it break in pieces and bruise" (verses 36-40).

The interpretation of the stone smashing the image at its toes is found in the 44th verse:

"And in the days of these kings shall the God of heaven set up a kingdom, which shall never be destroyed: and the kingdom shall not be left to other people, but it shall break in pieces and consume all these kingdoms, and it shall stand forever." The Stone is Christ and His world-ruling kingdom. The interpretation of the stone is given many places in the

Bible. "Jesus Christ of Nazareth . . . is the stone which was
set at nought of you builders, which is become the head of
the corner" (Acts 4:10-11).

And so we see that here are four universal world-ruling
gentile kingdoms. They begin with the Chaldean Empire,
which took the Jews captive to Babylon.

God had promised ancient Israel that if they would keep
His commandments, be His obedient nation, they would grow
into a multitude of nations—or an empire—that would dom-
inate the entire earth. But for disobedience they would have
to be taken captive by gentile nations (Lev. 26 and other
prophecies). Ancient Israel had been tried through the generations and centuries. They had disobeyed. Now they had been
taken captive by Nebuchadnezzar, who had raised up the
Chaldean empire. But as God revealed through Daniel in
chapter 2, it was God who had turned world dominion over
to this succession of gentile empires. They continue through
four great universal kingdoms and out of the fourth grows ten
succeeding governments. These carry to the time of the
Second Coming of Christ, and the setting up of the kingdom
of God to fill the whole earth and last forever.

The Fourth Beast

Plainly, here in Daniel 2 are described the same four universal world-ruling gentile powers that are described by Daniel's
four beasts. And this dream-image identifies who they are.
The first was Nebuchadnezzar's kingdom, the Chaldean Empire, called "Babylon" after the name of its capital city,
625-539 B.C.

The second kingdom, which followed, then, we know
from history, was the Persian Empire, 558-330 B.C., often
called Medo-Persia, composed of Medes and Persians.

All ancient-history students know the third world kingdom was Greece, or Macedonia under Alexander the Great,
who conquered the great Persian Empire 333-330 B.C. But
Alexander lived only a short year after his swift conquest, and
his four generals divided his vast empire into four regions:
Macedonia and Greece, Thrace and Western Asia, Syria and
territory east to the Indus river, and Egypt. So these were the
four heads of the third beast of Daniel 7.

And the FOURTH KINGDOM, which, developing from Rome, spread out and gradually absorbed one after another of these four divisions—"dreadful and terrible, and strong exceedingly," was the ROMAN EMPIRE (31 B.C. to A.D. 476).

It had absorbed all the others, occupied their territory, was greater and stronger than all. It included all the royal splendor of ancient Babylon, thus having the head—the strongest part—of the lion. It had all the massiveness and numerically powerful army of the Persian Empire—symbolized by the legs, the most powerful part of the bear. It was the greatest war-making machine the world had ever seen, and it also possessed the swiftness, the cunning, the cruelty of Alexander's army, symbolized by the leopard.

And thus, this fourth beast was unlike any wild beast of the earth. It was stronger, greater, more terrible, than any.

And so John, in Revelation 13, sees, not four beasts, but one beast. Not a leopard, but like a leopard—possessing all its cunning, cruelty and

THE IMAGE of Daniel 2 symbolized four world-ruling empires. C. Winston Taylor

speed. But it also possessed the dominant characteristics of
the two other most powerful beasts—the feet of a bear, and
the mouth of a lion. Daniel's fourth beast, the Roman Empire, had absorbed and therefore it included the three beasts
before it. Thus it included all seven heads. And John's beast
also has seven heads. It was Daniel's fourth beast, only, which
had ten horns and John's beast has ten horns.

And so, if we are willing to be guided solely by the Bible
description of this "beast" and to let the Bible interpret the
symbols used to describe it, we come to the inevitable conclusion that the beast of Revelation 13 is the Roman Empire,
of 31 B.C. to A.D. 476! Of course, many man-imagined theories,
widely taught and published, interpret this beast otherwise—
some as a church, some as a mysterious, individual, superman
yet to come. But these theories will not stand the test of
applying the Bible interpretation to all the symbols that
describe this beast.

Nebuchadnezzar's image, by the two legs, describes the
two divisions of the Roman Empire, after A.D. 330: West, with
the capital at Rome, and East, with the capital at Constantinople.

John also pictures this beast, not as a church or as an
individual man, but as a powerful government having a great
army. For they worshiped the beast by saying, "Who is able
to make war with him?" (Rev. 13:4).

The Symbolism of the Horns

Let us now notice the symbolism of the horns of the fourth
beast of Daniel 7 and of the beast of Revelation 13.

The ten horns symbolize the same thing—the ten stages
of government continuing out of the Roman Empire after its
fall, A.D. 476. The ten horns *"out of this kingdom"* (the
fourth—the Roman empire, 31 B.C. to A.D. 476) "are ten kings
that shall arise . . . and the kingdom and the dominion, and
the greatness of the kingdom under the whole heaven" (not
IN heaven) "shall be given to the people of the saints of the
most High" (Dan. 7:24, 27).

The ten horns, then, are ten kingdoms to arise *out* of the
fourth kingdom, the Roman Empire. These kings, also called
kingdoms, continue from A.D. 476 until the time when the

Stone, Christ and His Kingdom, smashes the image on its toes, and the kingdom is given to the saints. Therefore, since in actual history there have never been ten contemporaneous kingdoms that have continued out of the Roman Empire, side by side, down to the present—and since there have been nine successive kingdoms ruling that territory, which we shall explain, from 476 to the present, therefore we know that the kingdoms represented by the horns are successive, not contemporaneous.

The Deadly Wound

Now let us return to our description of the beast in Revelation 13.

"And I saw one of his heads as it were wounded to death; and his deadly wound was healed: and all the world wondered after the beast.

"And they worshipped the dragon which gave power unto the beast: and they worshipped the beast saying, Who is like unto the beast? Who is able to make war with him?

"And there was given unto him a mouth speaking great things and blasphemies; and power was given unto him to continue forty and two months" (Rev. 13:3-5).

The beast here symbolized is the one which included the royal splendor and kingly power symbolized by the mouth of the lion (Babylon); the ponderous strength symbolized by the feet of the bear (Medo-Persia); and the speed, cunning and cruelty of the leopard (Greece). Since the interpretation of these symbols is found in Daniel 7, and since the fourth beast had ten horns, the Bible interpretation of the beast of Revelation 13 is the fourth beast of Daniel 7—the Roman Empire, of 31 B.C. to A.D. 476. The beast described by John in Revelation 13 included 7 heads, but the only head existing at the time John saw this nondescript beast (which included the most powerful characteristics of all the beasts symbolizing its predecessors) was that of the fourth beast of Daniel, containing the seventh head, and also the ten horns. So the specific "one of its heads" that was wounded to death (Rev. 13:3) was the seventh head of the Roman Empire—the head out of which ten horns grew. The ten horns, as Daniel interprets, represent ten successive governments out of the Roman Empire, which were to continue until the setting up of the Kingdom of God at the Second Coming of Christ.

The deadly wound, then, was the one administered to the Roman Empire, when, in its last decaying stages, the barbarians overran it, ending its government in A.D. 476.

Notice, the dragon gave his power to the beast. Who is the dragon?

Some have said "pagan Rome." But will we be guided solely by the Bible interpretation of its own symbols? Then, if we will, the dragon is a symbol which means Satan, the devil. Notice Revelation 12. "The great dragon ... that old serpent, called the Devil, and Satan ... was cast out into the earth ... the devil is come down unto you, having great wrath ... and when the dragon saw that he was cast unto the earth ..." (verses 9, 12-13). "And he laid hold on the dragon, that old serpent, which is the Devil, and Satan ..." (Rev. 20:2).

They worshiped the beast (Rev. 13:4). Therefore some conclude, from this one statement alone, that the beast must be the papacy, not knowing that the people worshiped the Roman Empire and its emperors! Notice how they worshiped the beast—saying, "Who is able to make war with him?" The Roman Empire was the greatest war-making power the world had ever known. This beast killed by the sword (v. 10).

History is full of accounts of the worship of the Roman emperors, for paganism was a state religion. The following is from Robinson's *Medieval and Modern Times,* an older college textbook, page 7:

"The worship of the emperor: In a word, the Roman government was not only wonderfully organized ... everyone was required to join in the worship of the emperor because he stood for the majesty and glory of the dominion ... all were obliged, as good citizens, to join in the official sacrifices to the head of the state, as a god."

But when the seventh head of this great beast received its deadly wound in A.D. 476, was that the end? No, the prophecy says "his deadly wound was healed ... and power

---

THE APOSTLE JOHN was filled with great amazement when he beheld in a vision a woman riding a scarlet-colored beast having seven heads and ten horns (Rev. 17).   C. Winston Taylor

was given unto him to continue forty and two months" (verses 3, 5). The ten horns represent ten successive kingdoms to follow out of this kingdom. So, through the ten horns growing out of this head (the Roman Empire of 31 B.C.-A.D. 476), the beast (for the ten horns are part of the beast) continues until the Second Coming of Christ.

The text says one of his heads was wounded to death. The beast included the seven heads and the ten horns. John sees the beast living in the days of its seventh head, the Roman Empire. And when that head of the beast was suffering from its deadly wound, his—the beast's—deadly wound was healed. The horns now reign, one by one.

The Roman empire in Northern Africa was overrun by the Vandals, who sacked Rome in 455. Then in 476 Odoacer set up his government at Rome, called the Heruli. But it did not heal the deadly wound, for this was a government *in* Rome. It was not a Roman government, but one of foreign barbarians.

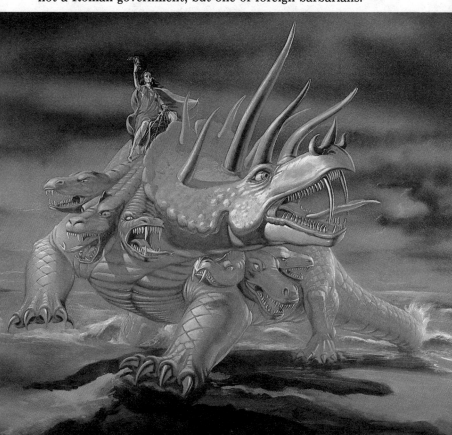

Then there was the kingdom of the Ostrogoths, 493-554, another outside foreign people who ruled in the territory. But they were driven out of Italy and disappeared.

These three kingdoms, sweeping into the Roman territory, filled the period known in history as the "transition age" (see Myers' *Ancient History*, page 571). That is, a TRANSITION between the wound and the healing.

Now Daniel saw a "little horn" coming up among these ten, before whom these first three were "plucked up by the roots" (Dan. 7:8). That leaves 7 horns to come. And of the little horn, Daniel 7 says "his look was more stout than his fellows" (verse 20). The papacy dominated completely all the horns to follow.

The Deadly Wound Healed

It was the fourth kingdom (symbolized by the fourth horn), succeeding the fall of the Empire in 476, which really HEALED the deadly wound, and restored the empire. In A.D. 554, Justinian, Emperor of the East, from Constantinople, set up his government through an Imperial Legate at Ravenna, Italy, and brought about what is known in history as the "Imperial Restoration" of the Empire.

Now, notice verse 5 of Revelation 13. Power was given to this beast, once healed, to "CONTINUE FORTY AND TWO MONTHS." In the prophecies pertaining to the times of Israel's punishment, each day represents a year in the actual fulfillment (Ezek. 4:4-6, Num. 14:34). Thus, the healed beast is to continue 1260 years.

Following the healing, in 554, came the Frankish kingdom (French), the Holy Roman Empire (German, then the Austrian Habsburgs) and Napoleon's kingdom (French). But when Napoleon was crushed in 1814, the healed beast continued no longer. "So closed," says West's *Modern History*, page 337, "a government that dated from Augustus Caesar" (from 31 B.C.). It went into the Abyss!

And from 554 to 1814, the duration of the "healed beast," was exactly 1260 years!

At that time, eight of the horns having appeared and gone, the beast itself went into the non-existent condition symbolized in Revelation 17:8 as the "bottomless pit." But by the year 1870, Garibaldi had united the many little divisions in the peninsula of Italy into one nation, and the kingdom thus established began the ninth horn, which culminated in the Fascist rule of Mussolini.

The "Heads" the Woman Rode

We shall deal later more specifically with the 17th chapter of Revelation in this connection. But let us note in passing that the woman mentioned in this chapter never rode on any part of this beast of Revelation 13 except its last seven horns! She is the "little horn" of Daniel 7, whose "look was more stout than his fellows," and who caused the first three to be plucked up by the roots. And since, in the 17th chapter of Revelation, the woman rode on all seven of the heads of the beast there pictured, and since she rode none of the heads but only the last seven of the horns of the 13th chapter beast, it follows that the seven horns of the "healed beast" of the 13th chapter form the seven heads of the beast of the 17th chapter!

Notice, at the time John saw the beast, five are fallen, one is, and one is yet to come (Rev. 17:10). The five that are fallen are the five during the 1260 years in which power was given, by religious authority, for the healed beast to continue. The one that "is," is the kingdom that extended from Garibaldi to the downfall of Mussolini. It was not in any sense the power-wielding old Roman Empire, so during the stage of this 9th horn (Rev. 13) or 6th head (Rev. 17) John speaks of it as the beast that was, and is not, and shall arise once more out of the bottomless pit.

The 7th head with its 10 horns, in the 17th chapter, will be, as the 17th chapter explains, the revival of the beast, the Roman Empire, "out of the bottomless pit" by a "United States of Europe," or federation of 10 European nations centered within the bounds of the old Roman Empire (Rev. 17:12-18). This is actually beginning today!

The entire beast of Revelation 17—the revivals of the Roman Empire—is a part "of the seven" heads of Revelation 13 and Daniel 7 because it comprises the last seven horns. Yet this revived Roman Empire is "the eighth" system, differing from the seven before it (Rev. 17:11).

The Number of the "Beast"—666—
Whose Number Is It?

Where shall we find that mysterious number 666? Does the pope, as some claim, wear it on his crown, identifying him as the beast of Revelation 13? Or must we look for it elsewhere?

Here are all the scriptures speaking directly of this number:

"And that no man might buy or sell, save he that had the mark, or the name of the beast, or the number of his name. Here is wisdom. Let him that hath understanding count the number of the beast: for it is the number of a man; and his number is Six hundred threescore and six" (Rev. 13:17-18).

"And I saw as it were a sea of glass mingled with fire: and them that had gotten the victory over the beast, and over his image, and over his mark, and over the number of his name, stand on the sea of glass, having the harps of God" (Rev. 15:2).

Note These Points

From these scriptures, we have the following definite points:

1. The beast has a number and may be identified, if we have wisdom, by this number.

2. The number is 666.

3. We are told to count this number—that is, add it up. The same Greek word is used elsewhere only in Luke 14:28: "count the cost."

4. This number, 666, is the number of the beast. The only Bible interpretation of this symbol, "beast," is a kingdom or the king who rules it and, therefore, really is the kingdom (Dan. 7:17-18, 22-24, 27). Therefore 666 must be the number of the KINGDOM, or GOVERNMENT, or EMPIRE, as well as that of the king who founds or rules it.

5. The expression "the name of the beast, or the number of his name" makes plain that the number 666 is the number of the name of the kingdom or empire.

6. The expression "it is the number of a man" shows we must also count this number in the name of the king, or ruler, over the kingdom identified as the "beast."

The Beast Is Not the Woman

In the 17th chapter of Revelation we find a beast, and a woman—a great, wealthy but fallen woman—who was riding the beast. The Bible describes the symbol "woman" to mean a church (see II Cor. 11:2; Rev. 19:7; Eph. 5:22-27). On the other hand, "beast" is a symbol of a kingdom, or empire.

Let us be consistent. The beast of Revelation 13 is not the woman who rode the beast—the beast is the government, and the woman is a church.

The beast of Revelation 13 is the Roman Empire!

This beast had a deadly wound (Rev. 13:3). That means the beast ceased altogether to exist or function as it had since 31 B.C. Yet its deadly wound was later healed, after which (verse 5) it continued to exist another 1260 years!

Those who believe a church is the beast say this deadly wound came in 1798. But the church did not cease to function in that year. Napoleon's abuse of the Pope in 1798 could in no sense be called a wound to death. And those who teach this do not expect that church to continue on another 1260 years.

The Founder of Rome

The founder and first king of Rome was Romulus. The Roman Empire was named after him. But the origin of the kingdom goes back to the time of king Lateinos, or Latinus in Latin, who founded the Latin kingdom four centuries before Romulus founded its future capital.

When John wrote this Revelation, telling us to count the number of the beast, he wrote in the Greek language. Consequently, we should look for this name, and the number 666, in this language recognized in the Bible, not in the Latin.

We are all familiar with the Roman numerals, where letters are used for numbers. All understand that I is 1, V is 5, X is 10, etc. But many do not know that the Greek language, in which the book of Revelation was written, also uses letters for numbers.

In the Greek, the language in which Revelation was written, the name of the founder of the kingdom was understood in the second century A.D. to have originally been spelled Lateinos. It signifies "Latin man" or "the name of

Latium," from which region the Romans derived their origin and their language. This word, too, signifies "Roman." In the Greek, L is 30, A is 1, T is 300, E is 5, I is 10, N is 50, O is 70, S is 200. Count these figures. They count to exactly 666!

It is indeed no coincidence that the name of the kingdom, its founder and first king, counts to exactly 666!

Certainly the beast stands identified!

And Mussolini, Too

The same number—666—was also associated with the man who dominated the puny sixth head of the symbolic beast.

Mussolini called himself "Il Duce." Italians shouted "Viva Il Duce!"—which means "long live the chief." Everywhere in Italy was the printed sign, "*vv il duce*." The "VV" is the abbreviation used for "Viva." A "V" is used instead of the "U" as is very commonly done. While this is a greeting, or title, Mussolini actually employed "Il Duce" as a name. Though it is Italian, the language is derived from Latin. So let's count it.

V is 5, V is 5, I is 1, L is 50, D is 500, V is 5, C is 100, E has no number. Now count them, and you have exactly 666.

Thus this number 666 was associated with the Roman Empire in this century.

But, some will ask, does not this number apply to the Pope? Some teach "the words 'Vicarius Filii Dei' are on the Pope's triple crown." The Pope does, on some occasions, wear a triple crown, but these words are not on it! We should be careful to prove all things.

Furthermore, these words are in the Latin, not a Bible language. This is not a name, but a title, and it is the name of the beast, and the number of the name of the man of the beast we are told to count. Further, this Latin title does not apply to a kingdom, or empire, but alone to a man.

And so the number 666 is branded on the Roman Empire, on the founder and first king of the Latins, on every Roman, and even on Mussolini.

Could anything be more conclusive?

The "Two-horned Beast"

Satan has his civil government on earth. He gave it "his power, and his seat, and great authority."

He also has organized religion as his instrument in deceiving the world. In II Corinthians 11:14, we find Satan is transformed into an "angel of light." According to Revelation 12:9 and 20:3, he has deceived the whole world. How?

Paul tells us in II Corinthians 11:13-15. Satan has his ministers who pretend to be the ministers of righteousness, but are actually false apostles, deceitful workers, calling themselves the ministers of Christ! Therefore they claim to be Christian ministers. They are the many, not the few, because all prophecies say it is the many, not the few, who have been deceived. Satan's main labor for six thousand years has been the deceiving of the world.

Now turn to the 13th chapter of Revelation, beginning with verse 11:

"And I beheld another beast coming up out of the earth; and he had two horns like a lamb, and he spake as a dragon."

THE FIRST TWO of four beasts that emerged from a turbulent sea in Daniel's dream (Dan. 7) are depicted in these illustrations.   C. Winston Taylor

Who—what—is this "beast"?

Some say it will be the United States aligned with the papacy. Some believe it is a federation of Protestant churches. Most church organizations ignore this very vital subject completely, or say frankly, "we do not know!"

Why this ignorance, when the answer is so plain? Yes, why indeed?

The Bible Interpretation

Remember, first, the Bible interprets its own symbols! When men put their own interpretation on Bible symbols, their conclusions are always false!

Notice, after John saw one beast, which we have proved to be the Roman Empire, he now sees ANOTHER—a different—beast rise up. We have learned that "beast" is a symbol for a kingdom, or civil government (Dan. 7:17, 23), and the term represents either the kingdom or its leader, as the case may be (Dan. 7:17, 23).

So this other beast with the two horns is the prophecy of another kingdom or government. In these prophecies, God pictures to us the earthly gentile governments as the wild beasts whose characteristics describe them. This two-horned beast appeared as a lamb. But actually it spoke as a dragon—its true characteristic—for "out of the abundance of the heart the mouth speaketh" (Matt. 12:34).

What does the word "lamb" symbolize, in the Bible? The answer is, Christ (John 1:29; Rev. 17:14). And "dragon" is a symbol of the devil (Rev. 12:9, 20:2).

So here is some kingdom or government appearing as that of Christ, or the Kingdom of God.

Christ did not set up a government (kingdom) at His first appearing on earth. After His resurrection the disciples asked Him if He would at that time restore the kingdom (Acts 1:6); but He did not. The Church is not the Kingdom. Because some thought it was, Jesus spoke the parable of Luke 19:11-27 to show that He first must ascend to His Father's throne in heaven to receive the royal power to become King of kings, to set up the world-ruling Kingdom of God. But Satan is a deceiver, and he has deceived the world into supposing his (Satan's) system of churches is the Kingdom of God.

Now notice carefully Revelation 13:12:

"And he exerciseth all the power of the first beast before him."

The first beast is the Roman Empire. Here is another government pretending to be Christ's government, the Kingdom of God, taking, exercising, using, employing, all the power of the first kingdom.

Now when? "He exerciseth all the power of the first beast before him, and causeth the earth and them which dwell therein to worship the first beast, whose deadly wound was healed" (verse 12). So, it was after the deadly wound (of A.D. 476) was healed. It was healed when Justinian brought about the restoration of the Empire in the West in A.D. 554. Consequently this religious government exercised power after A.D. 554 when the Roman Empire was restored.

So here we have pictured a government—a religious government—appearing as Christ's government, masquerading as the Kingdom of God, actually ruling the civil Roman Empire after A.D. 554.

The teaching in that day was that the Second Coming of Christ is fulfilled in the person of the leaders of the church. The millennium had begun.

For the entire 1260 years, the emperors acknowledged the supreme power of religion. The church was organized as a government—as a dual, two-fold government (symbolized by its two horns or kingdoms—for "horns" symbolize kingdoms also—see Dan. 7:24). It embodied church government, and it also was a state or civil government, always occupying a certain amount of territory over which it, alone, ruled as an independent sovereign state—in addition to actually ruling over the vast civil kingdom called the Holy Roman Empire. Even today, it is a separate, independent, sovereign state.

Notice, this second beast was to wield power over all the earth, because it was to cause the earth, and them that dwell therein, to worship this first beast "whose deadly wound was healed"—after 554.

In most any encyclopedia, under "Millennium," you will read the history of this very event—of how the "Holy Roman Empire" was called the "Kingdom of God upon earth." They claimed the Millennium had arrived!

Notice Revelation 13:14: "And deceiveth them that dwell on the earth by the means of those miracles which he had power to do in the sight of the beast." Verse 13 says "he doeth great wonders."

So notice these three points:

(1) This beast performs miracles.

(2) He performed them "in the sight of" the Holy Roman Empire, or the first beast.

(3) With them he deceived all nations.

All Nations Deceived

Where else, in the Bible prophecies, do we find these same identical facts?

First, note Revelation 17. Here is pictured a woman. In II Corinthians 11:2, Ephesians 5:22-27 and elsewhere, we learn that "woman" is a symbol for church. This woman is a fallen woman—an apostate church—pictured as ruling over many nations (Rev. 17:1, 15).

In verse 3, this false church is pictured sitting on a beast "having seven heads and ten horns." A woman riding a horse guides, controls, the horse. It does her bidding.

Notice, verse 18, she is "that great city, which reigneth over the kings of the earth." Notice, verse 2, the inhabitants of the earth have been deceived by this counterfeit Christianity. Also, Revelation 18:3, she has deceived all nations.

Next, notice II Thessalonians 2:3-4. The day of Christ—and the coming of Christ—shall not come, until there be a falling away, and a "man of sin" be revealed. He exalts himself above all that is called God. As God, he sits in a temple claimed to be the temple of God, showing himself to deceive people into accepting him as God. God is our holy Father. This final man, in a religious office, will claim the same title. This wicked man is to be destroyed at, and by, Christ's coming (verse 8). Notice verses 9-10: "Even him, whose coming is after the working of Satan with all power and signs [miracles] and lying wonders, and with all deceivableness of unrighteousness."

Here is an important religious figure prophesied to perform miracles and lying wonders, with which he deceives people everywhere.

At Armageddon

This deceiving religious ruler will still be active clear down to Armageddon and the Second Coming of Christ! In Revelation 16:13-16 are described three foul spirits. They come from the dragon which is the devil; from the beast, which is the civil Roman ruler; and from the mouth of the false prophet associated with him. "For," continues verse 14, "they are the spirits of devils [demons], WORKING MIRACLES, which go forth unto the kings of the earth and of the whole world, to gather them to the battle of that great day of God Almighty." And they are gathered, finally, at Armageddon! Note it! Yet future, the Roman ruler, as the Roman Empire, is again restored, along with a great religious leader—and all in the power and influence of the devil! Working miracles! All prophecies concerning them show these powers doing the same things!

Now notice the last battle of "the great day of God Almighty."

In Revelation 19:19-20 is pictured the beast—"and with him the false prophet that wrought miracles before him, with which he deceived them that had received the mark of the beast, and them that worshipped his image."

Note it! Compare with the two-horned beast of Revelation 13:11-17:

(1) Both perform miracles.

(2) Both perform them before, or in the sight of, the beast.

(3) With them, both the false prophet and two-horned beast deceive them that have the mark of the beast—cause them to receive that mark (Rev. 13:16).

Certainly, then, this two-horned beast, the false prophet, the man of sin and the woman that rode the beast are all picturing a counterfeit Christianity.

Did the two-horned beast deceive the very ones who have the mark of the beast? He did! Continue in Revelation 13:

"And deceiveth them that dwell on the earth"—how? " . . . saying to them that dwell on the earth, that they should make an image to the beast, which had the wound by a sword, and did live. And he had power to give life unto the image

A CHART SHOWING PROPHECIES OF REIGN OF GENTILE KINGDOMS

Dan. 2 The IMAGE	Daniel 7 The FOUR BEASTS (State)	Dan. 8 The RAM and GOAT	Revelation 13 The BEAST and IMAGE (Church)	Rev. 17 BABYLON and BEAST	EXPLANATION of Symbols	The EVENTS Fulfilled in HISTORY
Head of GOLD v. 32, 38	1st BEAST like LION v. 4				1st HEAD of prophetic BABYLON	The CHALDEAN EMPIRE (Babylon) 625-539 B.C.
Breast and arms of SILVER v. 32, 39	2nd BEAST (BEAR) v. 5	RAM with 2 horns v. 3, 4, 20			2nd HEAD of prophetic BABYLON	The PERSIAN EMPIRE (Medo-Persia) 558-330 B.C.
Belly and thighs of BRASS v. 32, 39	3rd BEAST (LEOPARD) 4 heads v. 6	HE GOAT with great horn and 4 notable ones v. 5-8, 21, 22			3rd, 4th, 5th, 6th HEADS of prophetic BABYLON	GREECE, under Alexander the Great, and four divisions, began 333 B.C.
Legs as IRON v. 33, 40-43	4th BEAST strong like IRON with 10 HORNS v. 7, 23, 24		The BEAST with 7 HEADS and 10 HORNS v. 1, 2		7th HEAD of prophetic BABYLON, with ten HORNS	The ROMAN EMPIRE, 31 B.C.-A.D. 476, in 2 divisions, West and East
			The DEADLY WOUND v. 3			Fall of the ROMAN EMPIRE A.D. 476
	1st HORN (plucked by roots)		1st HORN		These three horns, destroyed at behest of Pope, fill the "Transition Age" (Myers)	The VANDALS A.D. 429-533
	2nd HORN (rooted up)		2nd HORN			The HERULI, Odoacer's government, A.D. 476-493
	3rd HORN (rooted up)		3rd HORN			The OSTROGOTHS A.D. 493-554

Want To Know More?...

Enroll in
the Ambassador College
Bible Correspondence Course...

it's absolutely free!

(Details on other side) ▶

The Keys to Biblical Knowledge.

The *Ambassador College Bible Correspondence Course* isn't just a course about the Bible.

It's a course about life itself.

What is the purpose of life? Why is there evil in the world? What will happen in coming world events?

All these questions and many more are answered in the *Ambassador College Bible Correspondence Course,* and it's absolutely free of charge, with no obligation.

Each month you'll receive a complete lesson on a single topic of interest, with periodic quizzes to help you evaluate your own progress. And again, there is no tuition fee or obligation.

So request your introductory lesson today, and begin to discover answers to the big questions of life.

...24-27		v. 11-18	v. 1, 2	the GREAT	government
4th HORN		1st of remaining 7 horns—DEADLY WOUND HEALED (to continue 1260 years) v. 5	1st HEAD of BEAST (healed) ridden by scarlet-clothed woman	Since the "Great Whore" never rode any of the 7 heads of the 1st 4 beasts, but did mount and ride the last 7 horns of Daniel's 4th beast it follows that the last 7 horns of Dan. 7 and Rev. 13 are the 7 HEADS of Rev. 17 (5 fallen at collapse of Napoleon).	"IMPERIAL RESTORATION" of empire by Justinian, A.D. 554. He recognized supremacy of this world's Christianity.
5th HORN		2nd of remaining 7 HORNS	2nd HEAD ridden by woman		FRANKISH KINGDOM Began 774. Charlemagne crowned A.D. 800
6th HORN		3rd of remaining 7 HORNS	3rd HEAD ridden by woman		HOLY ROMAN EMPIRE (German head). Otto the Great crowned 962.
7th HORN		← 554-1814 = 1260 years beast continued → (4th of remaining 7 HORNS)	4th HEAD ridden by woman		HABSBURG dynasty (Austrian head), Charles V crowned 1530.
8th HORN		5th of remaining 7 HORNS	5th HEAD ridden by woman		NAPOLEON'S KINGDOM (French head), crowned 1804.
		In 1814, just 1260 years after "deadly wound" was healed, the "HOLY ROMAN EMPIRE" was dissolved. "So closed a government that dated from Augustus Caesar" (West, p. 377).			
9th HORN		6th of remaining 7 HORNS	6th HEAD ridden by woman	(One IS) Rev. 17:10	ITALY, united by Garibaldi, 1870 to 1945
10th HORN		7th and last HORN / Beast ascends out of pit	7th head and ten HORNS	(One yet to come)	Revived ROMAN EMPIRE, by 10 rulers under one leader.
The Ten TOES					

of the beast, that the image of the beast should both speak, and cause that as many as would not worship the image of the beast should be killed. And he causeth all, both small and great, rich and poor, free and bond, to receive a mark in their right hand, or in their foreheads: and that no man might buy or sell [trade, earn a living, hold a job], save he that had the mark, or the name of the beast, or the number of his name" (verses 14-17).

So, notice: This two-horned beast not only caused people to receive the mark of the beast (compare Rev. 19:20), but also perpetrated the forming of an image that caused the martyrdom of saints. As many as would not worship this image were caused to be killed. This false church did not kill them—she caused them to be killed. History shows that the civil government martyred millions who were declared "anathema from Christ" or "heretics."

Compare with the woman who rode the Beast in Revelation 17: "And I saw the woman drunken with the blood of the saints, and with the blood of the martyrs of Jesus" (verse 6).

Certainly these are one and the same.

Now this ecclesiastical organization, which is a twofold government, deceived the people by saying they should make an image of the beast. Note it (Rev. 13:14)—that is how it deceived people. What is an image? Dictionaries define it as a "likeness," or a "copy, representation, model, semblance, counterpart." So here is a church saying, "Let us make a model, or counterpart, of the civil Roman government"—for that is what the beast is.

Jesus Christ proclaimed the Kingdom, or government of God—divine government by will of God and by God's law—not paganized human government by will of man and man-made laws. His Church includes all Spirit-begotten saints who have and are led by the Holy Spirit. Christ is its only Head, and His Kingdom is not of this world!

Where, then, did human church government derive its present form? "The first pope, in the real sense of the word, was Leo I (440-461 A.D.)," says the *Cyclopedia of Biblical, Theological, and Ecclesiastical Literature,* volume 7, page 629. To him the form of government of the Roman Empire was the most marvelous thing on earth. He applied its principles

THE THIRD BEAST in Daniel's dream was followed by a fourth that was "dreadful and terrible" (Dan. 7).

C. Winston Taylor

to the church, organized the church into a government, forming the papacy.

This church government or organization is the image of the beast.

Says Myers' *Ancient History:* "During the reign of Leo I, the Church set up, within the Roman Empire, an ecclesiastical state [government] which, in its constitution and its administrative system, was shaping itself upon the imperial model." This church government, then, according to this historical authority, is in fact a model, a counterpart, an image of the beast which is the Roman Empire government.

The *Britannica* calls it an ecclesiastical world empire!

This image—man-designed and man-ruled church government—compelled people to worship the church! And since the church was organized into a worldly government, this was worship of the image—false worship—idolatry!

this church became a mother, and daughter churches
t of her in "protest," calling themselves "Protestant."
have worldly, political church government. "Upon her
l was a name written, MYSTERY, BABYLON THE GREAT,
THER OF HARLOTS" (Rev. 17:5). Her daughters are
harlots." Together, they are called "BABYLON." They
an, teaching pagan doctrines and customs, cloaked in
me of Christianity! And all nations are deceived!
s, human-organized churchianity, not Bible-designed
al-organism government, is the image of the beast. It
pagan political counterfeit of God's government.
Come out of her," God says (Rev. 18:4). God help us to

But let's look at all the facts God reveals on the subject—all the scriptures bearing on it.

WHOSE Mark?

Note this well! The "mark" is the mark of the BEAST—and the "beast" is the ROMAN EMPIRE. In Revelation 17 a later stage of this same wild beast is pictured, and there a "woman"—a great CHURCH—sits astride it, guides it, rules over it. But the MARK is the mark of the ROMAN EMPIRE—not the Roman Catholic Church.

That is fact number one. Keep that in mind.

Now in verse 11 of Revelation 13 *another* "beast" is pictured. This beast had two horns *like* a lamb, but spoke as a dragon.

This second beast of Revelation 13 is also pictured in Revelation 17 as the harlot woman who rode the beast. This fallen woman or church is different from all other churches in one respect. She is organized as a civil government, as well as an ecclesiastical church. Nations of the world send ambassadors to her, the same as they do the capitals of other nations.

This church, just as the woman riding an animal guides and directs the animal—like, for example, a woman riding a horse—took over, exercised, wielded, all the power of the first beast—the Roman Empire.

After A.D. 554, the church did do this for 1260 years, as prophesied!

Notice, further, Revelation 13:15-16:

"And he had power to give life unto the image of the beast, that the image of the beast should both speak, and cause that as many as would not worship the image of the beast should be killed. And he causeth all ... to receive a mark in their right hand, or in their foreheads" (Rev. 13:15-16).

Now here is a *deceived* church—both herself deceived by, and therefore used by the devil, and also *deceiving* the world. Notice, this church did not actually herself kill these martyrs—she merely *caused* them to be killed. And she it was, too, who CAUSES all under her domination to receive the dread MARK of the beast.

The Brand of Rome

Notice carefully what the above text tells us:

1) "He"—the leader who originated human civil government, modeled after that of the Roman Empire, in the
church.

2) *"Causeth"* all to receive this mark. It is the church,
not the civil government, which forces this brand on people.

3) It is the same power which *caused* the martyrdom of
saints.

4) It brands on the people the mark of the "beast"—that
is, the mark of the Roman Empire, *not* the mark of the
church.

5) This mark is received in the right hand, and in the
forehead.

So the MARK is that of the Roman Empire, which this
CHURCH did cause or shall cause the western world to receive.

TWO Martyrdoms

Next notice *when* these saints were killed. This will show
us *when* the mark of the beast is enforced.

"And when he had opened the fifth seal, I saw under the
altar the souls of them that were slain for the word of God,
and for the testimony which they held: and they cried with
a loud voice, saying, How long, O Lord, holy and true, dost
thou not judge and avenge our blood on them that dwell on
the earth?" (Rev. 6:9-10).

Here we find pictured the martyrs of the Middle Ages
already dead, at the time of this vision—which is the approx-
imate present. They know "Vengeance is MINE, saith the
Lord." They know God's judgments against this persecuting,
deceiving, false church, as described in Revelation 18, are to
be the seven last plagues, poured out "in the presence of the
Lamb" at the Second Coming of Christ. Read of it in Revelation 18.

These dead saints are pictured as crying out to ask "HOW
LONG" before the Second Coming of Christ and the seven last
plagues which will avenge their martyrdom. Foxe's *Book of
Martyrs* tells us that in the Middle Ages more than fifty
MILLION were killed, many for their BIBLE faith and obedience

to God instead of obedience to this church government of man and the devil. Notice, now, what must *again* happen *before* the seven last plagues and the coming of Christ!

"And white robes [symbolizing righteousness and purity] were given unto every one of them; and it was said unto them, that they should rest yet a little season, *until their fellow-servants also and their brethren, that should be killed as they were,* should be fulfilled" (Rev. 6:11).

Christ will not come to take vengeance on this great false church UNTIL *another* great martyrdom has taken place!

Note it! There was one martyrdom. Those saints are already killed. Their resurrection will occur WHEN Jesus returns to earth—WHEN His judgments are poured out on this false BABYLON and her daughter churches! But there is yet to be *another* universal persecution and martyrdom of saints, just prior to Christ's coming in vengeance against the forces of evil! Here are TWO universal martyrdoms!

This coming great martyrdom is THE GREAT TRIBULATION (Matthew 24:9, 21-22). This tribulation is not the wrath of God—the last plagues. It is the wrath of Satan (Rev. 12:12), inflicted at the behest of HIS apostate church *by* the coming "United States of EUROPE" and against the true people of GOD! It is a persecution—a torturing—a martyring of the saints of God—the very elect who cannot be deceived (Matt. 24:24). Except those days of Great Tribulation be shortened, no flesh would be saved. But, for THE SAKE OF GOD'S PERSECUTED SAINTS those days shall be shortened.

God shall intervene. Christ shall "come quickly."

The MARK Then, and Now

Now compare with these scriptures:

In Revelation 17, picturing this same church as the woman riding the beast, John writes: "And I saw the woman drunken with the blood of the saints, and with the blood of the martyrs of Jesus" (verse 6).

Also: Revelation 20:4—"And I saw thrones, and they sat upon them, and judgment was given unto them: and I saw the souls of them that were beheaded for the witness of Jesus, and for the word of God, and which had not worshiped the beast, neither his image, *neither had received his mark* upon their foreheads, or in their hands; and they lived and reigned with Christ a thousand years."

Now we see WHY these many millions were, and shall be, martyred! It was because they refused to receive this mark of the beast—refused to join in this worship of church and Empire! They obeyed God rather than man! Their lives were governed by God. They were called out of this world—no longer any part of this world. They were the children, the heirs, the future citizens of His KINGDOM, not the kingdoms of men. But—note it well!—they were, as God commands, subject to the government of MAN. They did not resist—they yielded themselves subject to the penalty. They were tortured—they were *killed!* But they obeyed the government of God rather than man where there was conflict. And, at Christ's coming to rule the world as KING of kings, they shall all be lesser priests and kings under Him and rule the world!

Do you see what this plainly reveals? Those martyrs, over a thousand years ago, were killed BECAUSE they would not worship the church, conform to its idolatry and pagan beliefs and customs, or worship the so-called "Holy Roman Empire"—and BECAUSE *they refused to receive the* MARK *of the beast!*

This means the MARK of the beast is something that was forced on people, on pain of being killed, *more than a thousand years ago!* The MARK of the beast was in full existence and enforcement over a thousand years ago!

BUT, since it is those who have the mark of the beast who shall suffer the seven last plagues at Christ's coming, the dread mark is once again to be enforced! And those who refuse it are those who shall be MARTYRED in the coming GREAT TRIBULATION!

Now we begin to find real light shed on this baffling question!

Warning of Third Angel

Soon, now, the time is coming when gross spiritual darkness will cover this earth—when no human will be permitted to preach Christ's true Gospel. We must work while it is day—the night is fast drawing on when no man can work for God.

At that time God shall send angels with His final warning to these apostate nations under sway of this great deceiving church as a final witness against them. Three such angel messages are foretold in Revelation 14. Notice the final warning of the third angel:

"If any man worship the beast and his image, and receive his MARK in his forehead, or in his hand, the same shall drink of the wine of the wrath of God"—the seven last plagues, full force, unmixed with mercy (Rev. 14:9-10)!

This shows that although the MARK was branded on all but the martyrs over a thousand years ago, it is STILL the brand of traditional Christianity today, and is ONCE AGAIN to be enforced. Once again those who refuse it shall be martyred. But those who receive it shall suffer the wrath of God without mercy!

You must soon choose whom *you* will obey—this coming Roman Empire resurrected by a United States of EUROPE, ruled by traditional Christianity—or whether you shall OBEY GOD!

A Mark of Obedience

We begin now to see that the MARK of the beast involves a point of OBEDIENCE—whether we shall OBEY GOD, or reject the commandment of God and obey MAN'S rule. It has something to do, then, with the COMMANDMENT OF GOD!

Notice, there are, in general, two classes—one has the MARK, the other rejects it and is martyred. Notice now the description of those who *refuse* this evil MARK:

"Here is the patience of the saints: here are *they that keep the commandments* of God, and the faith of Jesus" (Rev. 14:12).

There it is! In verses 9-11 of this chapter the third angel warns that those who have the mark of the beast shall be punished by the plagues of God. In the next verse, the 12th, the saints who do *not* have the mark are those who KEEP THE COMMANDMENTS OF GOD. Those who have the mark, therefore, are those who refuse to keep the commandments of God. The MARK of the beast, therefore, involves a rejection of the COMMANDMENTS OF GOD, or of one of them, for if we break one we are guilty of all (James 2:10).

So, one class of people accepts the MARK of the beast. The other class keeps the commandments of God.

A Mark of Disobedience

Hence, *whatever* the mark of the beast may be, it means disobedience to GOD'S government—to the commandments of God.

Here's further proof—here are they who get victory over this mark: Revelation 15:2-3: "And I saw as it were a sea of glass mingled with fire: and them that had gotten the victory over the beast, and over his image, and over his mark, and over the number of his name, stand on the sea of glass, having the harps of God. And they sing the song of Moses the servant of God, and the song of the Lamb, saying, Great and marvellous are thy works, Lord God Almighty; just and true are THY WAYS, thou King of saints."

This corresponds to the children of Israel, delivered from Egyptian bondage under Moses. Moses was a type of Christ. Pharaoh was the type and forerunner of this beast. The plagues God poured on Egypt were a type of the last plagues to be poured out on Babylon. The children of Israel stood on the shore of the Red Sea, and God miraculously delivered them. Here the saints of God are pictured on this symbolic sea of glass.

They sing the song of Moses, and the song of the Lamb (Christ). Moses pictures law and God's commandments; the Lamb (Christ) pictures faith and salvation from sin.

Remember, the beast is the human civil organization of the devil. In Revelation 12, we find Satan stirred to great wrath "because he knoweth that he hath but a short time" (verse 12). He then starts a great PERSECUTION, or TRIBULA-TION against the TRUE Church—the true saints of God. This is just prior to the Second Coming of Christ (verse 10). Now notice against whom Satan is so wroth:

"And the dragon [Satan] was wroth with the woman [Church], and went to make war with the remnant [last generation] of her seed, *which keep the commandments of God,* and have the testimony of Jesus Christ [the Bible]" (verse 17).

There it is again! Those keeping God's COMMANDMENTS

—those yielding themselves to God's RULE, and living by every Word of God—by the BIBLE—which *is* the written testimony of Jesus Christ—they are the ones the devil will persecute and martyr through his false church and his reborn Empire!

But Satan knows his own. He will brand his own with a mark, so they shall not receive this persecution and martyrdom, even as God put a mark on sinning Cain lest men finding him slay him (see Genesis 4:15). Those in the world who do *not* receive Satan's brand—the MARK of the BEAST—will suffer Satan's wrath in the Tribulation.

Thank God, those days shall be cut short, *for the elect's sake!*

Class on Whom Plagues Fall

There are TWO classes of people. That class which receives the MARK of the Beast is the class upon whom the PLAGUES OF GOD will fall. So if we can further identify those who shall receive this WRATH OF GOD, and *why* God will thus punish them, we shall further identify what the mark is.

In Ephesians 5 Paul is telling Christians to flee fornication, covetousness, idolatry—transgressing the TEN COMMANDMENTS. Then he says: "for because of these things [transgressing God's LAW] cometh the WRATH OF GOD [last plagues] *upon the children of disobedience*" (Eph. 5:6).

How plain! The wrath of God—the seven last plagues—is coming on those who DISOBEY God, by violating the commandments. The plagues fall upon those who have the mark of the beast!

Those who receive the plagues are breakers of God's commandments, and also at the same time receivers of the MARK! It becomes more and more plain that the mark of the beast represents COMMANDMENT-BREAKING.

Notice this again in Colossians 3:5-6: "Mortify therefore your members which are upon the earth; fornication, uncleanness, inordinate affection, evil concupiscence, and covetousness, which is idolatry [transgressions of some of the Ten Commandments]: for which things' sake the wrath of God cometh on the children of disobedience."

Notice it also in the prophecies of the Old Testament: "The great *day* of *the Lord* [time of God's wrath—the last plagues] is near.... That day is a day of wrath, a day of trouble and distress.... And I [God] will bring distress upon men, that they shall walk like blind men [the plagues! But *why?*], *because they have sinned* against the Lord ..." (Zeph. 1:14-17).

What is *sin?*

"Sin is the transgression of the law" (I John 3:4)—commandment-breaking.

The TRUTH Becomes Plain

Now, let's recapitulate! The truth is becoming plain!

1) The *mark* plainly means the rejecting and breaking of God's commandments. And in James 2:10-11, God says if we break only one of the commandments, we are GUILTY of breaking the LAW—guilty of all!

2) The Roman Empire is the real author of this *mark.* It is the mark of the BEAST, not the woman who rode the beast.

3) The church *caused* people to be deceived into receiving this *mark.*

4) Satan gave this Roman Empire its seat and great authority—it is the political instrument through which Satan works, in deceiving the world.

5) Those who refuse this *mark* are prohibited from "buying or selling,"—engaging in commerce, trade, or holding a job.

6) Many of those refusing this *mark* were, and shall again be, martyred because of their refusal—because they keep the commandments of God!

7) Therefore, the inevitable and plain conclusion is that the *mark* is something enforced by the church, originating in the paganism of the Roman Empire, which a cunning, deceiving devil would seize on as a means of cleverly DECEIVING people into breaking God's Ten Commandments. And it involves a direct connection with *holding a job*—engaging in business—earning a living.

Satan is clever—cunning—a deceiver. He palms off counterfeits, which look like the genuine! Naturally he would select the *one* commandment of God which he can counterfeit with a substitute—one in which by human reason alone no man could see where it would make any difference! He would select the one which would seem of least importance to the carnal human mind!

He would not try to deceive men on idolatry, profanity, or on stealing, lying, murder, adultery—though he has led people into all of these.

BEFORE DETERMINING exactly what the mark of the beast is, it is necessary to identify the beast itself as the apostle John described it in Revelation 13:1-7.

C. Winston Taylor

But WHAT commandment could it be—*what* commandment affecting a man's *job* or his *business?*

There is only one possible commandment—the one regarded by the largest number as the "LEAST" of the commandments—and that is the fourth commandment, which says: "REMEMBER the sabbath day, to keep it holy . . . The seventh day is the sabbath of the Lord thy God."

No carnal mind can see, without the special spiritual revelation of God through His Word, where it makes any difference WHICH day man observes.

WHERE DID SUNDAY ORIGINATE? Not with the church, but with the pagan religion of the ROMAN EMPIRE! It is the day on which the ancient pagans assembled at sunrise, faced the east (as they do Easter Sunday morning today) and worshiped the rising SUN. It was Constantine, emperor of the Roman Empire, not a pope, who made SUNDAY the official so-called "Christian day of rest." But it was *enforced*—people were *caused* to accept it universally—by the CHURCH!

Why Saints Were Martyred

It was for obeying God's FOURTH Commandment—keeping the Sabbath—that millions were put to death. The local Council of Laodicea, about A.D. 363, passed this decree: "Christians must not Judaize by resting on the Sabbath, but must work on that day, rather honoring the Lord's Day, resting then as Christians. But, if any shall be found Judaizing, *let them be anathema from Christ*" (*Nicene and Post-Nicene Fathers,* vol. XIV, p. 148).

The church *caused* them to be killed. When the church branded one "anathema" (a heretic), the state began torturing him. Unless he recanted, he was tortured until he died! Laws became so strict no man could hold a job, or engage in business, unless he worked on Saturday and rested on Sunday. And the world will be so geared that it will be almost impossible for one to "buy or sell" except he receive this MARK OF THE BEAST!

This is the ONLY COMMANDMENT which was altered by the Roman Empire! In Daniel 7:25 we read the prophecy of this BEAST and the little horn (the political government of the church) rising up, which was to think to CHANGE "times and laws." That is, change God's LAW in respect to TIME—the time for the Sabbath!

What Is a Mark, Anyway?

Now what *is* a "mark"? In Bible usage it is virtually synonymous with a "sign," and in one or two places used interchangeably. There is merely this difference: A "mark" is a brand of identification, forced on one. Cattle raisers put by force their mark on their cattle—their brand. A "sign" is also a badge of IDENTITY, but one voluntarily accepted and used. A druggist hangs a sign in front of his store. It may say, "JONES & CO., DRUGS." It *identifies*. It tells what kind of store, and who owns it.

Now the beast, in association with the church, used FORCE to brand the Western world with their MARK. Those who obeyed God and kept His Sabbath were martyred. They were unable to "buy or sell." But God does not force anyone. God lets us make our own decision about obeying Him, accepting Christ and becoming His obedient children.

But is the Sabbath God's SIGN that we are Christians, belonging to HIM?

God's SIGN

Yes, indeed! It was *after* God had made, and ratified, the covenant with Israel. That Old Covenant, of course, was for limited duration and is now replaced with the New. But any covenant made *after* it had been made and ratified by blood *was no part of that Old Covenant.*

It was forty days after that ratification that God made a new, separate, different covenant between Himself and all who should be His people, to last *forever*. This was no temporary covenant, but for all generations, FOREVER.

It is found in Exodus 31:12-17:

"And the Lord spake unto Moses, saying . . . Verily MY SABBATHS ye shall keep: for it is a SIGN between me and you *throughout your generations.*" These generations of Israel (see our free booklet *"The United States and Britain in Prophecy,"*) *are still going on!*

Now WHY is it a sign? Does it IDENTIFY God to us? Does it *identify* us as HIS? " . . . that ye may know that I am the Lord that doth sanctify you."

Get the powerful meaning of those words!

It is a SIGN, that we may KNOW that the Eternal is the true God. It identifies who God is. How? Notice verse 17: "It is a SIGN ... for in six days the Lord made heaven and earth, and on the seventh day he rested, and was refreshed." It is the memorial of God's rest from CREATION. Always, in all parts of the Bible, God identifies Himself as CREATOR. How can we distinguish who is the TRUE God, from all the false gods?

The true God *created* everything that is, including everything from which people have *made false* gods. Some worshiped the sun. But the Eternal, the true God, created the sun, and rules it. Some worship idols carved out of stone, or wood, or marble. But the true God *created* that from which they were made, and even the human beings who made them. The Sabbath is GOD'S Sabbath, not the Jewish Sabbath. Never does the Bible call it the "Jewish Sabbath." It identifies GOD as the CREATOR.

The Sabbath was made FOR MAN. So said Jesus (Mark 2:27). It was made WHEN man was made (Genesis 2:1-3). It was MADE—and it was Christ, the Yahweh or Eternal, who made it! Therefore HE is Lord of the Sabbath! It was made to keep man in the true knowledge of the IDENTITY of the true God, to keep him from idolatry! And history proves that every nation that did NOT keep God's Sabbath worshiped false gods, and did not know who the true God was! When Israel quit keeping God's Sabbath, they went into idolatry (Ezek. 20:5, 11-13, 17-21).

It was for SABBATH-BREAKING GOD SENT BOTH ISRAEL AND JUDAH INTO SLAVERY!

But back to Exodus 31:17-18. It also is the SIGN by which we are identified as belonging to GOD. We BELONG to whom we obey—so we read in Romans 6:16! It is the *sign* by which we know He is the ETERNAL ... "that doth sanctify YOU." To sanctify is to set apart for spiritual use. The SABBATH sets one apart from the world, and always did—as OBEYING and belonging to GOD. Can you think of ANY REASON why anyone would EVER keep the Sabbath, except to OBEY GOD? Would any man defy human custom and invite persecution, and be set apart as different, through human reason?

Could any atheist be a Sabbath keeper? THE SABBATH IDEN-
TIFIES GOD'S PEOPLE!

God's people, we have seen above, are identified as they
who KEEP THE COMMANDMENTS. The *world* acknowledges all
the other nine commandments. The only one the world
rejects is the fourth. The only one that sets one apart from
the world—that IDENTIFIES one as belonging to GOD—that is
a SIGN of God—is the SABBATH.

Notice, verse 16, it is a "PERPETUAL COVENANT." *It is a*
COVENANT! It is no part of the Old Covenant—no part of the
law of Moses! It was made with Israel *after* all these, and is
a separate, and *perpetual* COVENANT.

Notice verse 17: "It is a SIGN between me and the
children of Israel FOR EVER." There it is! It is a COVENANT. It
is FOREVER!

When given to physical, flesh-born Israel, this covenant
punished by death any breaking of the SIGN. Today, since the
administration of the death penalty by the Levites and judges
is not being done (II Cor. 3:7-8), and since all believers, in all
nations, whether Israelite or gentile, are grafted into *spiritual*
Israel (Romans 11:24), the willful refusal to keep this *sign* is
punishable by death—*the second death*.

"He that despised Moses' law died without mercy under
two or three witnesses: of how much sorer punishment,
suppose ye, shall he be thought worthy, who hath trodden
under foot the Son of God . . . ?" (Heb. 10:28-29).

On Right Hand and in Forehead

God says the penalty for SIN is DEATH! Sin is the transgression of the law. If we break only this one commandment, we
are guilty. The penalty is DEATH!

The Roman church caused people to receive the MARK of
pagan ROME—the Sunday observed by the pagan Roman
Empire—and the penalty for disobedience was DEATH!
Fifty million or more were put to death—so says history.

The Sabbath commandment is the ONLY commandment
the world will not accept in its MIND (forehead) and OBEY (by
work, or rest, with the HAND). It is the ONLY commandment
that can distinguish between those who have the MARK of the
BEAST, or the SIGN OF GOD.

Now the book of Revelation is written mostly in symbols. The right hand symbolizes work or labor—the forehead, the intellect or mind. It has to do with what we BELIEVE, in the mind, and whether we OBEY, with the hand.

HOW ABOUT GOD'S SIGN? *It also was received in the forehead, and the hand!*

Regarding one of God's annual Sabbaths, we read: "... it shall be for a SIGN unto thee *upon thine hand*, and for a memorial *between thine eyes* [forehead], that the Lord's LAW may be in thy mouth" (Ex. 13:9).

Deuteronomy 6:1, 6-8: "Now these are the COMMAND-MENTS ... and these words which I command thee this day, shall be in thine heart ... and thou shalt bind them for a SIGN *upon thine hand*, and they shall be as frontlets *between thine eyes*."

Deuteronomy 11:18: "Therefore shall ye lay up these my words in your heart and in your soul, and bind them for a SIGN *upon your hand*, that they may be as frontlets between your eyes."

Also see Proverbs 7:2-3 and Revelation 7:3-4; 14:1.

There is absolute proof! Yes, the truth is very plain!

The Sabbath is God's SIGN, standing, more than any commandment, for OBEDIENCE. It was symbolically in the HAND and in the FOREHEAD, just as the MARK of the BEAST—the pagan SUNDAY—was in the right HAND and in the FOREHEAD!

SUNDAY observance—Christmas, New Year's, Easter, etc.—*this is the* MARK of the BEAST!

The church *did* cause all under the "Holy Roman Empire" to receive this mark, during the Middle Ages. Not only were active church members caused to observe Sunday instead of the SABBATH, but it became a universal custom so that all the Western world—regardless of religious connection or belief, accepted Sunday instead of SATURDAY as the weekly day of rest. It has become universal in the Western world except for Judaism, Islam, a few sects in Christianity, and the comparative few whom God has called out of this world and into His true Church.

Has she stopped?

Just at present she has not the POWER to enforce this

mark on everyone. But there will be a United States of EUROPE—a union of ten nations. It will be a UNION OF CHURCH AND STATE—and the church once again will sit astride "The BEAST."

Now notice Daniel 7:21-22: "I beheld, and the same horn [papacy] made war with the saints, and prevailed against them; *until* the Ancient of days came [Second Coming of Christ] and judgment was given to the saints of the most High."

Yes, the MARK OF THE BEAST once again will be *enforced!* No one will be able to hold a job or engage in business without it. Those refusing will once again be tortured and martyred—probably *by* the secret police of the political state—but at the behest of the church!

Today, ALL NATIONS are deceived by this paganism masquerading under the name "Christianity."

Today, America, Canada, Britain—Israelitish nations descended from the ancient so-called lost ten tribes of Israel—are actually *in* the ways of this "BABYLON."

God's *last warning* is this: "COME OUT of her, my people, that ye be not partakers of her sins, and *that ye receive not of* HER PLAGUES" (Rev. 18:4)!

IF you are branded by this MARK, *rejecting* the SIGN of God in your forehead and hand, you shall be tortured by God's plagues without mercy! Yes, YOU!

But if you OBEY God—if you are *watching*, praying without ceasing—you shall be accounted worthy to ESCAPE—and come under GOD'S PROTECTION (Luke 21:36).

A Unique Course Understanding

Have you found it difficult—even impossible—to understand what the Bible says? The Ambassador College Bible Correspondence Course can help you begin to comprehend the Bible as never before. More than 2,000,000 people have enrolled in this unique course!

These informative, eye-opening lessons make plain the answers to the "unanswerable" problems facing millions today. They explain the very purpose of human life. You will study the plain truths of your Bible!

You will learn the truth about the purpose of life, about what Bible prophecy says concerning world events today, about the God-inspired way to true happiness. All these topics and more are presented in step-by-step detail. A different major subject is explored in each monthly lesson.

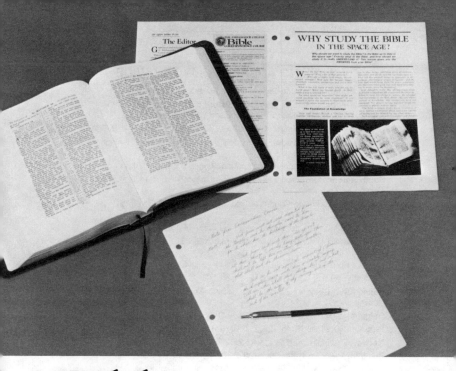

in Bible

And the Bible itself is the only textbook you will need.

You will find each lesson richly rewarding, and periodic quizzes will help you evaluate your progress. There is no tuition fee or obligation—these lessons are absolutely free! Why not request a sample lesson? Send your request in the reply envelope or write to our address nearest you.

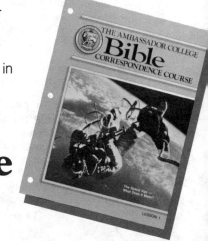

Free of Charge

Just mail the reply envelope stitched into this booklet.

MAILING ADDRESSES WORLDWIDE

United States: Worldwide Church of God, Pasadena, California 91123

United Kingdom, Europe (except as listed) and Middle East: The Plain Truth, P.O. Box 111, Borehamwood, Herts, England WD6 1LU

Canada: Worldwide Church of God, P.O. Box 44, Station A, Vancouver, B.C. V6C 2M2

Canada (French language): Le Monde à Venir, B.P. 121, Succ. A, Montreal, P. Q. H3C 1C5

Mexico: Institución Ambassador, Apartado Postal 5-595, 06502 Mexico D.F.

South America: Institución Ambassador, Apartado Aéreo 11430, Bogotá 1, D.E., Colombia

Caribbean: Worldwide Church of God, G.P.O. Box 6063, San Juan, Puerto Rico 00936-6063

France: Le Monde à Venir, B.P. 64, 75662 Paris Cédex 14, France

Switzerland: Le Monde à Venir, Case Postale 10, 91 rue de la Servette, CH-1211 Genève 7, Suisse

Italy: La Pura Verità, Casella Postale 10349 I-00144 Roma EUR, Italia

Germany: Ambassador College, Postfach 1129, D-5300 Bonn 1, West Germany

Holland and Belgium: Ambassador College, Postbus 444, 3430 AK Nieuwegein, Nederland

Belgium: Le Monde à Venir, B.P. 31, 6000 Charleroi 1, Belgique

Denmark: The Plain Truth, Box 211, DK-8100 Aarhus C, Denmark

Norway: The Plain Truth, Postboks 2513 Solli, N-0203 Oslo 2, Norway

Sweden: The Plain Truth, Box 5380, S-102 46, Stockholm, Sweden

Finland: The Plain Truth, Box 603, SF-00101 Helsinki, Finland

Australia: Worldwide Church of God, P.O. Box 202, Burleigh Heads, Queensland 4220, Australia

India: Worldwide Church of God, P.O. Box 6727, Bombay 400 052, India

Sri Lanka: Worldwide Church of God, P.O. Box 1824, Colombo, Sri Lanka

Malaysia: Worldwide Church of God, P.O. Box 430, Jalan Sultan, 46750 Petaling Jaya, Selangor, Malaysia

Singapore: Worldwide Church of God, P.O. Box 111, Farrer Road Post Office, Singapore 9128

New Zealand and the Pacific Isles: Ambassador College, P.O. Box 2709, Auckland 1, New Zealand

The Philippines: Worldwide Church of God, P.O. Box 1111, MCPO, 1299 Makati, Metro Manila, Philippines

Israel: Ambassador College, P.O. Box 19111, Jerusalem

South Africa: Ambassador College, P.O. Box 5644, Cape Town 8000, South Africa

Zimbabwe: Ambassador College, Box UA30, Union Avenue, Harare, Zimbabwe

Nigeria: Worldwide Church of God, PMB 21006, Ikeja, Lagos State, Nigeria

Ghana: Worldwide Church of God, P.O. Box 9617, Kotoka International Airport, Accra, Ghana

Kenya: Worldwide Church of God, P.O. Box 47135, Nairobi, Kenya

Mauritius: The Plain Truth, P.O. Box 888, Port Louis, Mauritius

THIS BOOKLET IS PROVIDED FREE OF CHARGE BY THE WORLDWIDE CHURCH OF GOD IN THE PUBLIC INTEREST. It is made possible by the voluntary, freely given tithes and offerings of the membership of the Church and others who have elected to support the work of the Church. Contributions are welcomed and gratefully accepted. Those who wish to voluntarily aid and support this worldwide Work of God are gladly welcomed as co-workers in this major effort to preach the gospel to all nations.

358177/8903
GAC